Contemporary Hand Made

TURKISH CARPETS

UĞUR AYYILDIZ
Art Historian and Professional Guide

NET®
TURİSTİK YAYINLAR SANAYİ VE TİCARET A.Ş.

Cover: Hereke, natural silk prayer rug.
Back cover: 1- Silkworms and mulberry leaves.
2- Dyed hanks of silk yarns.
3- A carpet motif pattern.
4- Different knotting systems.
5- Carpet-weaving girl. `

1	2	
3	4	5

Published and distributed by:

NET TURİSTİK YAYINLAR A.Ş.

Yerebatan Caddesi, 15/3,
34410 Cağaloğlu, İstanbul-Turkey
Tel.: (90-1) 520 84 06 - 527 42 70
Telex: 23264 acı tr

1363. Sokak, No. 1, Kat: 5,
35230 Çankaya, İzmir-Turkey
Tel.: (90-51) 12 30 01 - 25 38 61

Sedir Mahallesi, Gazi Bulvarı,
Akdemir Apt., Kat: 1, D.6-7, Antalya-Turkey
Tel.: (90-31) 16 08 41

Yenimahalle, Nev-Yap Sitesi,
5. Blok, D.1, Nevşehir-Turkey
Tel.: (90-4851) 30 89

Text: Uğur Ayyıldız
        Art historian and professional guide
Layout: Not Ajans
Printed in Turkey by: Keskin Color Matbaası

ISBN 975-479-033-7

19th Edition, 1989

3

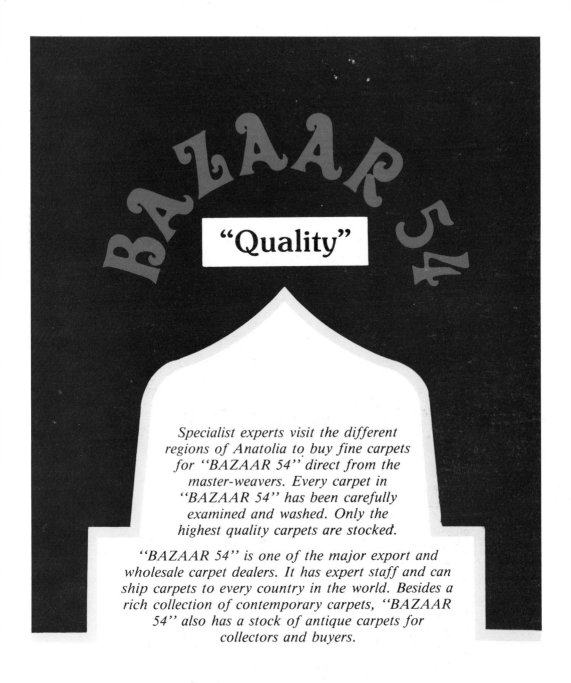

BAZAAR 54

"Quality"

Specialist experts visit the different regions of Anatolia to buy fine carpets for "BAZAAR 54" direct from the master-weavers. Every carpet in "BAZAAR 54" has been carefully examined and washed. Only the highest quality carpets are stocked.

"BAZAAR 54" is one of the major export and wholesale carpet dealers. It has expert staff and can ship carpets to every country in the world. Besides a rich collection of contemporary carpets, "BAZAAR 54" also has a stock of antique carpets for collectors and buyers.

CARPET

5

Hereke, natural silk carpet

Contents

Edremit pure wool "Çeyrek"

Preface

Precious handmade carpets are the products of long months of labor requiring great skill and patience. Besides being utilitarian objects, they are a source of pleasure to their owners.

A beautiful carpet is like a fine painting; it holds the eye. It is also an investment which will retain its value as the years pass.

Contemporary Turkish carpets are made by local masters who use materials and designs characteristic of the region in which they work. After careful checking for quality and a first washing, these carpets enter the domestic and foreign markets through the hands of famous dealers.

This catalogue is an illustrated guide to contemporary Turkish carpets region by region.

Carpet - weaving loom

INTRODUCTION

Until recent times all artifacts had to be handmade, but modern technology and mass production have replaced skills and techniques traditional for thousands of years. In our day handmade works are rare, and among them are the beautiful and functional knotted carpets made using traditional methods developed for over 2000 years.

Carpets, whose weaving can take months or even years of skill and effort, are pieces that can be kept and handed down from one generation to another, gaining in value as their antiquity increases. Each region has its own techniques and traditional designs practiced by its anonymous artists.

Carpet weaving and making is collective work using skills passed on for generations. Families, tribes, or even whole villages work collectively, pooling their special skills, knowledge, and expertise. The methods of manufacture and the different raw materials used produce distinctive carpets, characteristic of the region in which they are woven.

Handmade knotted carpets are used for various purposes by the local people in their region of origin. Besides being used as rugs, carpets serve such purposes as tent screens, paintings, cradle and sofa covers, wall hangings, and prayer rugs.

A beautiful high-quality handmade carpet increases in value as it is used; for the carpet's knots tighten in use, making it more brilliant and treasured.

Private collectors, distinguished families, and museums are proud owners of antique carpets. The richest collections of antique knotted handmade carpets are to be found at the Istanbul Museum of Turkish and Islamic Arts, the Vakıf Carpet Museum in the Blue Mosque, and the Konya Mevlana Museum. The museums and collectors of Europe and the USA own some exquisite pieces, most of which have been exported from Turkey. During the 14th, 15th and 16th centuries, handmade Turkish carpets were prized possessions of the noble and wealthy families of Europe. Carpets of this era, which have survived, have taken their places in museums.

For the last century or more, handmade knotted carpets have been a subject of research for experts and art historians. Great numbers of books and journals have appeared on the subject, showing that the making of handmade carpets is an important art form. The spread of knowledge through such publications has caused an increased demand for fine carpets.

Authorities conclude that the making of knotted carpets, produced in an area extending from the Mediterranean coast of Turkey to the steppes of Central Asia, was introduced by Turkish nomadic tribes and craftsmen. Traditional Turkish carpet making with its distinctive techniques, materials, patterns, and knotting has had a great influence upon all oriental carpets. In art history books, one comes across carpets that date back to the ancient Persian, the Pharoahs, and the Calips. However, these were not knotted carpets, but were rugs woven using the simple "towel technique" instead of knotting.

The hard-wearing double-knotted carpets are the invention of Turkish tribes. The techniques found in handmade carpets were brought to the Mediterranean coast by the Seljuks in the 12th century. Marco Polo mentions rich exhibits of carpets in palaces and mosques. Carpet making has developed at different speeds in different periods according to demand, but high-quality handmade carpets have always found a ready market.

Carpets are textile products; Turkish handmade carpets have always had patterns which fitted the specific nature of the materials and the knotting used. Another special characteristic of Turkish handmade carpets is the use of the double knot, known as the Turkish or Gördes knot. Although designs and patterns change and develope,the Turkish carpet always retains its historical and traditional features.

Material and technique

The carpets shown in this book are knotted handmade rugs woven mostly by the womenfolk of the regions.

The first step in carpet making is to have a pattern or a design. Master weavers do not need a pattern outline, but retain the pattern in their memories. The second step involves the choice of material. Materials used differ according to type and region. The material of a carpet may be wool, pure silk, floss silk, or cotton. The pure silk of Turkish carpets is produced from the cocoons grown in Bursa, one of the few silk centers of the world. Silk carpets are ideal ornaments, and may be used as tapestry, wall hangings, and for other decorative purposes.

The material most commonly used is sheep's wool. The Anatolian plateaus are excellent grazing land for sheep and good grazing land determines the sheen and strength of the wool.

Cotton is used in the weaving of a base (warp and weft) for the carpet and wool is then knotted on to this to form a pile. Carpets made with cotton and wool are as hard wearing, beautiful, and attractive as other carpets.

In carpets manufactured only in the Kayseri region, floss silk, which is a kind of artificial vegetal silk, is used. Floss silk makes up the pile knots of the carpet's cotton base system. It is as strong as other materials and is also easily dyed, making possible the production of a wide range of colors.

Flock of sheep on high-plains

Knotted carpets are woven on a loom consisting of horizontal bars on which the warp and weft threads are stretched. Onto these threads the pile knots are tied according to a pattern. The thread ends which make up the pile are clipped off so as to get a velvet-like soft surface. Thus the motifs are made up of thousands of individual knots. The tighter the knots, the finer and stronger is the carpet. The pleasure one gets from a beautiful carpet equals the pleasure one gets from a beautiful picture.

The double knot, known as the Turkish or Gördes knot, is used in all typical Turkish carpets. Another well-known system is the Sehna or Persian knot. The Turkish knot is wrapped around two warps and the Persian knot around a single warp. A kilim, which is similar to a carpet, is woven on the loom but with a different technique; knots are not used and it is woven normally.

The Gördes knot makes a carpet stronger, firmer and more durable, while the Sehna knot allows the weaving of varied patterns. However, once a carpet is made it is difficult to determine the knotting system.

Raw wool market

Spinning of wool thread on spindle

Kettles used in dying

The colors also are characteristic of the region where the carpet is made. The threads used in the weaving of antique carpets were used to be dyed with natural dyes known only by the family that manufactured the carpet. Today chemical dyes are used along with vegetal dyes. Natural dyes are produced from leaves, roots, and fruits. Many of the villages engaged in carpet making have a grazing land called "Boyalık". Plants from which dyes are produced are grown there. The various formulas for dye production have been passed down from generation to generation. Thus the colors traditional to Turkish carpet making have survived till our day. Red is dominant in Turkish carpets. This striking color expresses wealth, joy and happiness. Green

Dyed wool hanks

sybolizes heaven; blue nobility and grandeur; yellow is believed to keep evil away, and black symbolizes purification from worries.

Turkish (above) and Persian knotting systems

Handmade carpets are generally called after the region or town where they are manufactured. Contemporary carpets are made in various sizes and with combinations of various materials. In some regions, the threads used in weaving and the knots may be only wool, and in some other regions, the base may be cotton and the knots wool. In other regions pure silk is used in the weaving of carpets.

Dimensions and nomenclature

Handmade carpets that can be used as rugs, wall hangings, and divan covers are manufactured in various sizes. Different names are given to carpets of different sizes. Although the names given according to size are the same for all regions, the carpets, because they are handmade, may show minor differences of dimension. While some regions manufacture carpets of all sizes, others manufacture carpets in standard sizes. Whatever the size is, a handmade carpet brings beauty and elegance to the place where it is used. Two or three handmade carpets laid over wall to wall carpeting will add color to the rooms.

Standard dimensions in centimeters :

Small yastık (pillow)	40 x 25
Yastık	100 x 60
Çeyrek	135 x 90
Seccade (prayer rug)	180 x 120 - 200 x 130
Karyola	220 x 150
Kelle	300 x 200
Taban	over 6 sq. meters
Yolluk (runner)	different sizes

Kayseri natural pure silk prayer rug

Buying a carpet

Handmade Turkish carpets are useful functional objects as well as investments for the future. When choosing among a wide range of exquisite carpets, the first criterion is falling in love at first sight. The carpet must fascinate and enrapture the buyer. However, quality is also very important, and that can vary greatly. A reputable expert dealer will carefully choose beautiful high-quality carpets and keep an extensive stock.

Handmade carpets are generally used as rugs, or as wall hangings. For a beautiful and long life, constant care is as important as the original quality. Carpets are brought to market after a special washing. Carpets which are cleaned regularly keep their bright and attractive sheen. The pile of the carpet attracts dust easily. The use of a vacuum cleaner will take away all the dust. If there is a long interval between cleanings, beating the carpet on the reverse side with a properly constructed flat reed beater is another good method that can be used. When cleaning the pile, sponge it with soapy water (not detergent). The best way to clean a very dirty carpet is to send it to a specialist carpet cleaner. When not in use, carpets should be rolled (not folded) and covered.

Kayseri floss silk runner

Carpet weaving centers

Technically, Turkish handmade carpets may be classified as Anatolian carpets. The carpets produced in towns and villages, and by the "Yürük" nomads reflect their art tradition. However, personal feelings and taste of the weaver may be reflected along with the traditional patterns. Handmade carpets contribute a lot to the budget of the family. Almost every region of Anatolia still produces great numbers of hand-made carpets in the traditional ways, making up beautiful collections. The village folk weave carpets characteristic of the region on the looms in their houses. Besides such local centers, carpet weaving has become an industry in certain cities and towns.

High-quality handmade carpets are manufactured in houses, private workshops, or in institutions subsidized by the government. The products of these centers display a rich variety of color, design, and size. The demand for handmade carpets can only be met by the production from these centers.

The carpet weaving centers and regions and the different materials used in those centers are shown on the map on the opposite page:

Handmade carpet weaving centers of Turkey

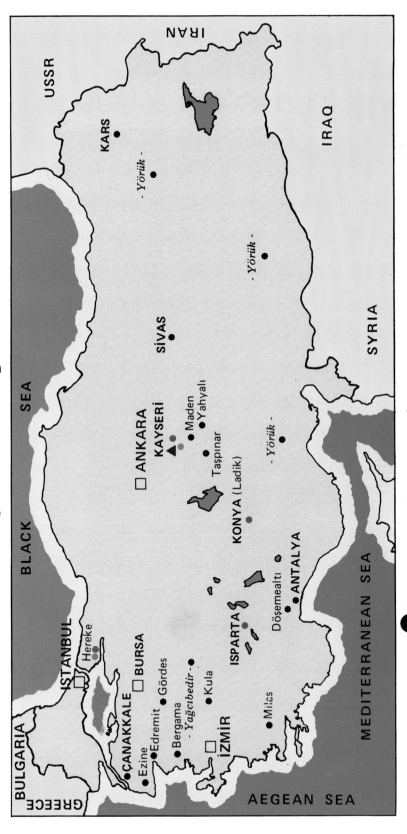

Centers that produce pure wool carpets
Centers that produce pure silk carpets
Centers that produce floss silk carpets
Centers that produce carpets with a cotton base and wool knots
Yörük (Nomadic) pure wool carpet regions

HEREKE

Hereke pure silk prayer rug

Hereke pure silk "Çeyrek"

The most famous and finest pure silk carpets of the world are produced in the small town of Hereke, 60 km east of Istanbul. Pure silk carpets made here are unrivaled in wealth and quality.

Since the 19th century, Hereke has been one of the most important carpet weaving centers. The first looms were installed by order of the Sultan for the making of carpets for the palace, the nobility, and important people. On these looms expert craftsmen of exceptional ability create valuable masterpieces full of charm. Naturalistic floral decoration is typical of the pure silk Hereke carpets. Plum blossoms, tulips, carnations, roses, and other flowers create an atmosphere of spring. With a million knots per square meter, the natural silk Hereke carpets represent the supreme achievement of contemporary carpet weaving. Some of the carpets are brocaded in gold thread. Besides pure silk carpets made from the silk produced in Bursa, Hereke is also famous for its wool carpets.

Natural silk carpets are manufactured in various sizes, they may be as small as a table mat, or big enough to be a piece of tapestry. Hereke wool carpets, on the other hand are for use in living rooms, dining rooms, and bedrooms.

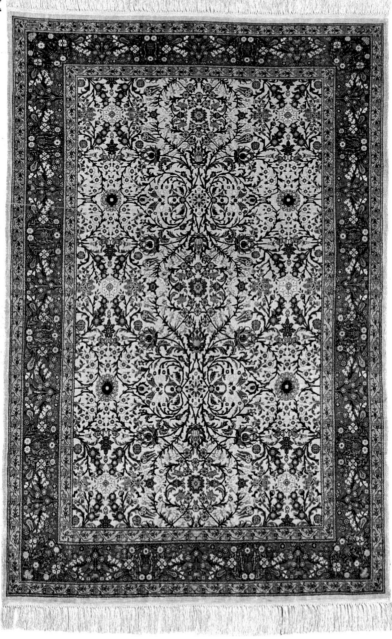

Hereke pure silk prayer rug

Room decorated with pure silk Hereke carpets

Hereke pure silk prayer rug

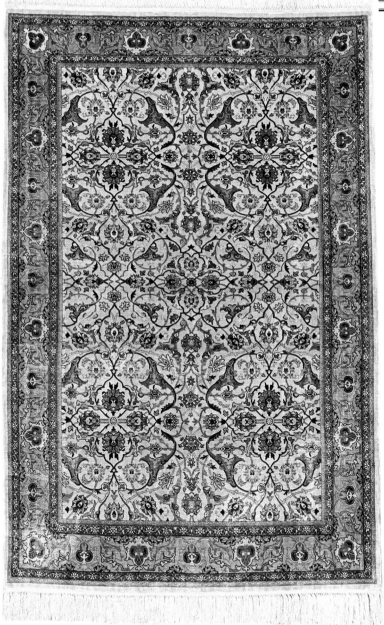

Hereke pure silk prayer rug

Hereke pure silk "Çeyrek"

Hereke pure silk prayer rug

Hereke pure silk "Yastık"

Hereke "Taban" carpet with cotton base and wool knots

Hereke "Taban" carpet with cotton base and wool knots

Room decorated with Hereke "Taban" carpet

KAYSERİ

Kayseri natural pure silk "Karyola"

Kayseri floss silk runner

The town of Kayseri, which is the capital of Cappadocia situated in Central Anatolia at the intersection of caravan roads, is one of the most famous carpet manufacturing centers of Turkey. Here carpets are produced using a variety of techniques and materials. The thousands of looms are an important source of income for the town itself and the nearby villages. Kayseri is the only center where carpets of all sizes are manufactured. Kayseri and Hereke are world centers for best quality natural silk carpets. The carpets made with the natural silk produced in Bursa are very bright in color and very decorative. Fine knotting and close pile make every detail of the design clearly visible. The same characteristics are found in the floss silk carpets produced in Kayseri. The handmade carpets produced with floss vegetal silk are very attractive and display excellent color harmony. With their various sizes, they suit homes decorated according to both classic and modern styles. These carpets adorned with traditional floral design fill the home with joy and create an atmosphere of a heavenly garden.

The floss silk Kayseri carpets have started a new era in carpet world and have become increasingly popular in European and American markets.

The wool Kayseri carpets produced in large sizes are available in different colors and designs. Some Kayseri carpets are also known as "Bünyan" carpets, after a nearby town.

Kayseri natural pure silk "Çeyrek"

Kayseri natural pure silk prayer rug

Kayseri floss silk prayer rug

Kayseri floss silk "Çeyrek"

Kayseri floss silk runner

Kayseri floss silk prayer rug

Kayseri floss silk prayer rug

Kayseri floss silk carpet lying in front of a bar

Kayseri "Taban" carpet with cotton base and wool knots

West Anatolian pure wool carpets

Çanakkale-Ezine pure wool carpet

Çanakkale-Ezine pure wool carpet

Çanakkale-Ezine

Classic design predominates in the pure wool carpets produced in the traditional style in and around the Dardanelles region and the shores of Hellespont. Certain vegetal colors and geometric patterns, characteristic of the carpets of the Aegean region are also typical of the carpets of the Çanakkale region, but patterns reflecting the personal feelings of the weaver may be added to the classical designs. The patterns consist of lozenges, squares, rectangles, and triangles, that esthetically cover the carpet. A few other decorative shapes are placed alongside or among these patterns. The bright colors which are used may be seen in the colorful local costumes. The carpets of the region are made of pure wool.

BERGAMA

Bergama pure wool "Çeyrek"

Bergama pure wool "Çeyrek"

One of the most famous names of ancient carpet weaving centers. Pure wool carpets of this region still have the tradition of ages. Geometric patterns, red color, and limited standard sizes are features of Bergama carpets.

EDREMİT

Edremit, pure wool "Çeyrek"

Edremit pure wool "Çeyrek"

The soft and very decorative Edremit carpets are made of pure wool. They are characterised by delicate colors and the geometric patterns which were brought to this region by emigrants from the Caucasus. The colors of these carpets are the colors of the local countryside; greens and yellows, especially olive and light lime, combine beautifully with shades of red. These carpets, which are manufactured in limited sizes, are becoming increasingly well known as the years go by.

YAĞCI BEDİR

Bedroom decorated with Yağcıbedir pure wool carpet

The pure wool Yağcı Bedir carpets produced in the mountain villages of the Aegean region are some of the best quality of their kind. The dominant colors of these very soft carpets are dark blue and red. The deep blue of the Aegean gives the basic color. This is patterned with geometric forms, stylized birds, and numerous stars of Solomon, and framed in a border of five or seven bands.

The warp, weft, and knots of the carpets are made of pure lambswool. The short clipped knots cause the pattern to be easily seen on the pile. This beautiful West Anatolian carpet is always produced in its unchanging colors and patterns.

Yağcıbedir pure wool runner

Yağcıbedir pure wool prayer rug

Yağcıbedir pure wool prayer rug

Yağcıbedir pure wool runner

Yağcıbedir pure wool prayer rug

KULA

Kula pure wool "Karyola"

Kula pure wool "Çeyrek"

The production of handmade carpets in Western Anatolia and the Aegean has a rich tradition and history. These carpets have been exported since 16th century and are generally known by the names of Kula or Izmir. They were used in churces and palaces. Sometimes one sees examples in the pictures of famous painters. Many of the classical old style hotels of the west were decorated with carpets from the Aegean region. The majority of the examples which have survived to our time are considered to be rare pieces and are kept in museums.

Today many carpet weaving centers outside the Aegean region make pure wool carpets in the traditional Kula patterns. These carpets provide the best examples of the Turkish art of carpet making and make one of the best souvenirs, since they can be handed down from generation to generation. They are manufactured in all sizes and colors.

Kula pure wool "Çeyrek"

Kula carpet decorating bar corner

Kula pure wool "Çeyrek"

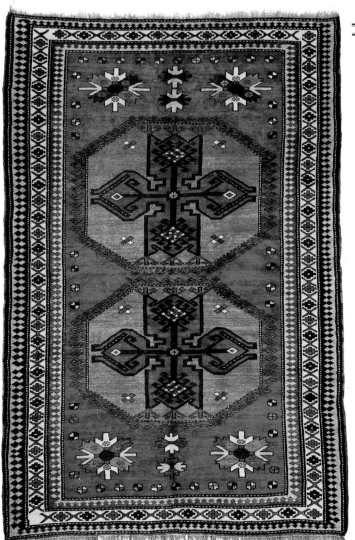

Kula pure wool "Çeyrek"

Kula pure wool runner

Kula pure wool "Çeyrek"

Kula pure wool "Çeyrek"

MİLAS

Milas pure wool prayer rug

Milas pure wool runner

The Milas carpet with its varied colors and compositions has an important place in Western Anatolian carpet production.

Instead of the colors used in the antique pieces, contemporary Milas carpets are made in pale, delicate tones produced with vegetal dyes.

The warp, weft and knots are pure wool. The dominant colors are yellow, the color of tobacco, dark and light brown, and reddish brown.

The geometric patterns which suit the production of pure wool carpets are the predominant design; another characteristic feature is the use of the "mihrap" (prayer niche) pattern.

Milas carpets are manufactured in limited sizes.

Milas pure wool "Çeyrek"

Milas pure wool prayer rug

Milas pure wool "Çeyrek"

Room decorated with Milas wool carpet

DÖŞEME ALTI

Döşemealtı pure wool "Çeyrek"

Döşemealtı pure wool "Çeyrek"

The Yürüks, who are seminomadic tribes, live throughout the winter on the warm plains. These seminomadic tribes manufacture handmade carpets, Döşemealtı, from the pure wool and vegetal dyes they themselves produce. The villages around Antalya, the Turkish Riviera, are the center of this type of carpet making. The design reflects the nomadic taste, which is expressed in geometric patterns, and a color harmony of blues, dark greens, and reds.

Döşemealtı carpets are made in a limited range of sizes.

Döşemealtı pure wool "Çeyrek"

Döşemealtı pure wool carpet in kitchen

Room decorated with carpets of different regions

Döşemealtı pure wool runner on staircase

Döşemealtı pure wool runner

Carpet weaving in central Anatolia

Yahyalı pure wool "Karyola"

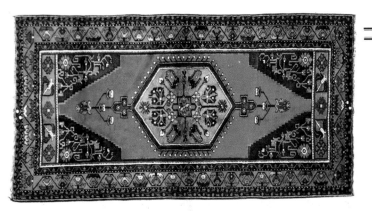

Yahyalı pure wool "Karyola"

Volumes of books are required to describe all the carpets produced in the cities, towns and villages of Turkey. Volumes have already been written about antique Turkish carpets, but a similar amount is required for contemporary Turkish carpets. Therefore, only a few examples of each region have been mentioned. However, it should be noted that no photograph can reflect all the reality and brilliance, beauty and luster of a handmade carpet. Kayseri, one of the main centers of this region, was introduced in the previous pages. Carpets with different features and characteristics are manufactured in Kırşehir, Avanos, Ürgüp, Niğde, Maden and other centers. Sometimes the characteristics differ from one village to the next only a few kilometers away.

YAHYALI

Yahyalı carpets are produced in a very small region. Pure wool and vegetal dyes are used in the making of Yahyalı carpets. These carpets, adorned with stylized floral patterns and geometric designs, are famous all over the world. Manufactured in villages, they reflect local colors and the use of high-quality materials. The artists produce their own materials for weaving and dying. Dominant colors of a Yahyalı carpet are navy blue, red and brown; other colors are placed among these. The major designs of a "mihrap" or a medallion are elaborated with the addition of geometric patterns. Yahyalı carpets are manufactured in a limited range of sizes.

Yahyalı pure wool carpet

Yahyalı pure wool "Seccade"

MADEN

Maden pure wool "Seccade"

Maden pure wool carpet

Another series created by pure wool threads and vegetal dyes. The main color is red and the designs are woven in soft colors. Geometric designs are enlivened with the addition of stylized floral patterns. The characteristic design is that of a medallion and a "mihrap". Maden carpets are manufactured in a limited range of sizes.

79

TAŞPINAR

Taşpınar pure wool "Seccade"

Taşpınar pure wool prayer rug

Taşpınar carpets, made of high-quality wool and vegetal dyes, are manufactured in a small region. Yellow frames the center of the carpet. Other dominant colors are bright red, navy, or dark blue. The borders bearing geometric patterns are enriched with the addition of stylized floral and rosette patterns. Taşpınar carpets are manufactured in a limited range of sizes.

KONYA-LADİK

Konya "Taban" carpet with cotton base and wool knots

Konya-Ladik "Taban" carpet, ideal for large rooms

The oldest known carpet making center in history is Konya. Marco Polo mentions the existence of workshops under the patronage of the Seljuk Sultans during the 13th century. Rare pieces from that century are exhibited in the carpet museums in Istanbul and Konya.

The Konya-Ladik carpets with their high quality various sizes, soft colors, and fine knotting are rare pieces always in demand in the carpet markets of the world. The carpets manufactured in Konya and the nearby town Ladik are contemporary copies of antique carpets.

Konya-Ladik carpets with their cotton base and wool knots are very popular, and suit tastes of all kinds. These carpets come in different sizes that can be used in living rooms and large spaces. Generally, natural dyes are used in the production of Konya-Ladik carpets. The dominant colors of these high-quality carpets are mostly soft hues displayed in tasteful combinations.

Konya "Taban" carpet with cotton base and wool knot

Konya "Taban" carpet with cotton base and wool knot

Konya "Taban" carpet with cotton base and wool knot

Konya-Ladik "Taban", goes with every style of decoration

Konya "Taban" carpet with cotton base and wool knot

Konya "Taban" carpet with cotton base and wool knot   89

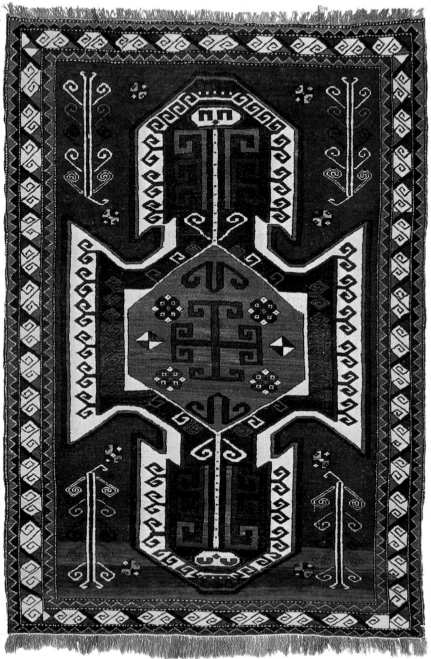

Kars pure wool "Kelle"

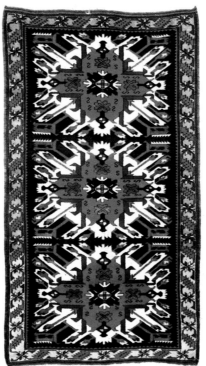

Kars pure wool "Kelle"

The mountainous regions, with fertile plateaus and the production of yarn that lasts for ages, are excellent areas for the making of knotted carpets and kilims. In every valley and every town of the region, carpets of various types are manufactured. Carpets for use in the home are loosely knotted. Besides these, high-quality and very fine pure wool carpets, also known as Yörük (Nomadic) carpets, are made here.

KARS

The carpets of this region are very distinctive and popular. Pure wool and vegetal dyes are used in their making. The geometric patterns predominant in the carpets of the region are of Caucasian origin.

They are manufactured in a limited range of standard sizes.

Kars pure wool "Karyola"

Kars pure wool "Karyola"

Kars pure wool "Karyola"

Kars pure wool "Karyola"

PUBLICATION LIST

ISTANBUL (B)
(In English, French, German, Italian, Spanish, Arabic, Greek, Turkish)
ISTANBUL (BN)
(In English, French, German, Italian, Spanish, Japanese)
ISTANBUL (ORT.)
(In English, French, German)
CONTEMPORARY HANDMADE TURKISH CARPETS
(In English, French, German, Italian)
HAGIA SOPHIA
(In English, French, German, Italian, Turkish)
THE KARİYE MUSEUM
(In English, French, German, Italian, Turkish)
THE TOPKAPI PALACE
(In English, French, German, Italian, Spanish)
THE SACRED RELICS
(In English, French, German, Turkish)
THE SÜLEYMANİYE MOSQUE AND ITS ENVIRONMENT
(In English, French, German)
Unique CAPPADOCIA-The Göreme Region
(In English, French, German, Italian, Spanish)
CAPPADOCIA (BN)
(In English, French, German, Italian)
ANTALYA (BN)
(In English, German)
ALANYA
(In English, French, German, Turkish)
ASPENDOS
(In English, French, German)
PERGE
(In English, French, German)
TRABZON
(In English, German, Turkish)
PERGAMUM
(In English, French, German)
EPHESUS
(In English, French, German, Italian)
PAMUKKALE (HIERAPOLIS)
(In English, French, German, Italian, Turkish)

TURKISH CARPETS
(In English, German)
The Capital of Urartu: VAN
(In English, French, German, Turkish)
VIDEO CASSETTE-Istanbul (VHS-Beta)
(In English, French, German)
COLOUR SLIDES *(36 different sets, 12 slides in each sets)*
THE MAPS OF TURKEY AND ISTANBUL CITY PLANS

Publications distributed by NET

EPHESUS (AT)
(In English, French, German)
LYCIA (AT)
(In English, French, German)
KARIA (AT)
(In English, French, German)
NEMRUT (AT)
(German)
EPHESUS (T)
(In English, French, German, Italian, Spanish)
PERGAMUM (T)
(In English, French, German)
EPHESUS (İA)
(In English, French, German)
PAMUKKALE (İA)
(In English, French, German)
TURKEY (İA)
(In English, French, German)
ANTALYA (İA)
(In English, German)
CAPPADOCIA (İA)
(In English, French, German)
TOPKAPI (İA)
(In English, French, German)

NET. BOOKSTORES

ISTANBUL,
1. Yerebatan Caddesi, Şeftali Sokağı, 10, 34410 Cağaloğlu
2. Ramada Hotel, Ordu Caddesi 226, 34470 Laleli
3. Ataköy Turizm Merkezi - Ataköy
İZMİR,
Cumhuriyet Bulvarı, 142/B, 35210 Alsancak